The Complete Guide to Curing Meat, Fish, Veggies, Nuts, Grains & More!

Learn the 8 Most Effective and Proven Dehydration Methods

Recipes with Easy-to-Follow Instructions

Miriam Howard

GALICIA
PUBLISHING HOUSE

Published by: Galicia Publishing House

Support@BarberryBooks.com
Design & Cover by Olivia O'Neal
First Edition

TABLE OF CONTENTS

INTRODUCTION

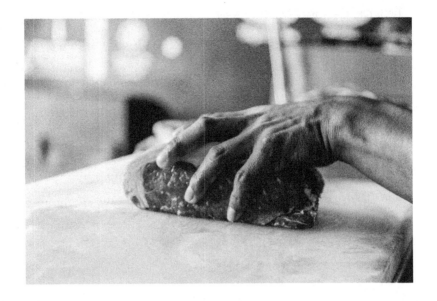

It has been said that water is the essence of life. It's the element that keeps our body functioning properly so that we can keep on living, and the same is true with other living organisms on the planet. However, there are some exceptions to the rule. Growing up near the woods of Colorado with parents who hunt, I learned at a young age how removing moisture can make food last longer and concentrate flavor.

Dehydration is both a culinary technique and a way to preserve. Dehydration allows us to forage for crops or animals in season and eat them in the off-season. It also allows us to buy bargain items in bulk, and make them last for a long time.

With today's price inflation, it simply makes sense for us to stretch out our food. Reducing food waste allows people to squeeze out all of the benefits from our resources and put them to good use.

These are hard times that we face. We must keep sustainability in mind to tide us over this period. I know that not all people can hunt or establish a farm to feed themselves. However, we can add dehydration techniques to our repertoire, and apply them to the food that we buy from the market.

This will allow us to survive more price inflation and the times when we can't get or buy food. It's also a good time-saver since food can be bought in advance and stored until needed-- days, weeks, or months later. You can even portion it into the amounts needed, so that you won't need to take out too much and risk spoilage.

So, dry off your hands, prune up, and let's go deep into the world of dehydration!

FOOD FOR DAYS, AND NO WASTE IN SIGHT

I don't want to sound like a doomsayer or like I'm part of a doomsday cult, but our ecosystem is in decline. No, the planet will not implode anytime soon, but it's slowly deteriorating. Think of it more like a cycle. Everything leads to entropy, but if given enough time, it will lead back to negentropy.

In this millennium, we are experiencing climate change, pandemic outbreaks, financial crises, and other problems. Man-made or not, these factors affect us to different degrees. That is why it's more important in these modern times to secure food sustainability.

At the national level, governments are looking to research better food production, alternative sources, and proper distribution of goods. They continuously manage the distribution of the limited amount of land area and energy available for food production on a monthly or yearly basis.

They monitor the greenhouse gas emissions of the food industry and look for more ways of bringing them down to a tolerable level. Food sustainability is an uphill battle against many external factors. It's a tough fight, but it's an adapt-or-die situation. We can also aim for food sustainability within our own households, but we have to do it ourselves.

Sustainability does not necessarily mean going vegan or living off scraps for the betterment of the environment. Well, the environment is part of it. Sustainability is about practices that are viable for an extremely long time and have minimal or no impact at all. Sustainability involves environmental, financial, political, and social factors.

When it comes to food sustainability, production, processing, transportation, and marketing are involved. It does not matter if the product has the cleanest production and is distributed via electric vehicles, if the general public can't afford to buy the product, then it's not a sustainable practice.

Food sustainability in our homes entails consuming as much food as we can, with as much nutrition as we can get, yet still operating within a budget. Notice that I said consume, not just get or procure. It's not sustainable to buy lots of food when half of it just ends up spoiled or thrown away.

This is where the knowledge of food dehydration or other forms of food preservation comes in. Practice allows us to enjoy food more, and for longer.

A 2016 study found that out of the total food produced, 30% of it was discarded as waste. It may not sound like a lot, but when you consider that the total amount of food produced that year was 200 million metric tons, that is equivalent to 60 million metric tons of food waste.

Now, it's accepted that not every morsel produced is edible, but all things being equal, it's still a lot. Considering the resources and energy consumed to produce the ingredients to make the food, transport it, and the emissions this entails, quite a lot of damage is done. This is compounded when you consider that 30% of the food just goes to waste.

The study attributes the high percentage of food waste to poor meal planning, poor understanding of when food is still good enough to eat, and underappreciation of the food industry. The thing is, we can have food sustainability and produce less food waste quite easily. It just takes a bit of know-how, forethought, and discipline.

So, here are some easy tips and basic lessons to get yourself on the road to food sustainability.

✓ Understand shelf-life labels properly. The United States Food and Drug Administration (FDA) requires these labels to ensure the safety and quality of products when the buyers consume them. However, some of these are just guidelines, and the edibility of the food can be left to your own judgment. If you have stored a product properly, like in the fridge or freezer, it can last way past the stated shelf life. Here are some terms used and what exactly they mean:

o **"Use by"** is for items that are totally unacceptable to be eaten after a certain amount of time, and under certain conditions, like meat and fish. However, if properly preserved, we can go beyond that, which is the main topic of this book, but more on that later.

o The **"best buy"** label refers to the optimum quality of that item, as recommended by the producer or manufacturer. You can actually still eat it past the date, but the quality may have changed.

o Chocolate bars may have light discolorations, which is just the cocoa butter separating from the cocoa solids. Juices will have some solids settling at the bottom, or cookies just become drier and crumbly. It may not look as intended, but it's still good to eat.

o The **"sell by"** date is for the sellers, to determine if the item should be replaced by newer stock. If you have bought an item before the sell by date, you still have a third of the product's recommended shelf life, so you can take your time.

✓ Items close to sell by or best buy date should not be discarded hastily. Use your well-informed judgment. My initial test is usually the smell. If it does not have any offensive aromas, then it should be safe to cook and eat. Know your ingredients as well. If it's marinated and has a good amount of salt, that typically gets rid of most harmful organisms, and actually cures the food item. Another tip is to know how to store it. If it's kept away from light, oxidation, air, and warm temperature, then it will mostly be fine. I have kept some bacon in the freezer for about two years, and it was still as good as the day I got it.

✓ Consider buying from your local farmers' markets. These items should be cheaper as it takes less to transport them, as you are buying directly from the farmer or producer. Also, if there is less transport and handling time, the produce is usually less damaged. This is why imported products cost a fortune.

✓ Support sustainably produced food, to ensure that the items are grown, produced, and processed in a sanitary environment, and in a safe manner for both the products and the consumers. These are usually food items produced without the excessive use of antibiotics or harmful pesticides, and produced outside of FDA, Department of Agriculture (DA), or other governing bodies.

✓ Having mentioned the last tip, read up on genetically modified organisms or GMOs. They usually get a bad rap from people who do not know what a GMO really is. It's basically a controlled evolution, not something grown out of a test tube, as some people would lead you to believe. Specimens of a product are bred to combine desirable traits into a single plant. This is why we have multi-colored cauliflowers, orange carrots, or large purple eggplants. Gene modifications are meant to make crops or other food products grow bigger, faster, and more fit for human consumption. Some specimens are even modified to tailor-fit the final product they are grown for, like cornstarch, sugar, and canola oil. So, make a place for them in your fridge or pantry. You may have already bought GMO products and not even known it.

✓ Sustainable farming and GMO factors all lead to lessening the environmental impact of making the product. So, choose food items produced with this in mind. This includes eating more vegetables. No, I'm not saying that you go full vegetarian or vegan, but just go with less meat, particularly beef and lamb.

✓ The meat industry makes up about 57% of the total greenhouse gases produced by the whole food production industry. Also, next to fossil fuels, agriculture is the largest contributor to the global greenhouse gases count. This is due to land conversions, transportation, and the resources it takes to feed animals.

✓ These things are compounded by the same factors just to grow the crops needed for feed. So go easy on the meat and replace it with some eggs (chicken produces the least greenhouse gases out of all meat production industries), beans, nuts, and fish.

✓ Speaking of fish, sustainable seafood is quite tricky. It varies depending on the source. Seafood tends to thrive in certain areas and can even vary by season and year. For these, always check the Ecolabels or certification from the Marine Stewardship Council (MSC), which states whether a particular type of seafood is currently sustainable and the best choice to eat.

✓ Also, check the Seafood Watch website which recommends sustainable seafood, and whether you should choose the farmed or wild-caught variety from a certain area. It's also good practice to always get what is local to you, or at least close by, to lessen transportation distance.

✓ Food is a necessity for a lot of households, and for life, essentially. However, it's apparent that we also have the capacity to overconsume. For years, we have been pointing fingers at fast food restaurants for expanding serving sizes, or raising the sugar content, which makes people crave more. And yes, the industry is partly to blame. However, we, as consumers, are on the other side of that coin. We demand and want more food to consume. Food

15

production is a business, so satisfying our hunger is a priority.

✓ It's an endless cycle. If we work just as hard as the food producers in maintaining our weight to a justifiable and reasonable level, the producers can ease up, and produce fewer food products. This entails less processing time, fewer emissions, less waste, less pollution, less transportation, and less fuel consumption. The simple act of maintaining a healthy weight will ripple far into the world of food sustainability.

✓ There are instances of a particular food deemed sustainable and good to eat, causing people to flock to consume that particular product. The thing is, most people only concentrated on that product and not much else, swinging the pendulum over to making it unsustainable. This happened to squid, bananas, and beef. Overeating only a certain product causes the demand to go up, which translates to more producers acquiring land, which leads to over-cultivation, just to keep up with demand. So, it's highly recommended to diversify your diet and meal plans.

✓ There is no escaping the fact that we eat with our eyes. We see something that looks good and tasty, and we crave it. Companies spend millions a year on advertising and product design, so that when we walk through the grocery aisles, we are severely tempted to buy their products. This leads to impulse buying. There are lots of homes which throw away food that was bought due to impulse buying. Creating a meal plan will allow you to buy the food items that you want in the right amount, thus decreasing food waste. It may take some time from your daily or weekly tasks, but meal planning will lessen food waste, and will even save you some cash.

✓ Consider walking off the beaten path, and consuming food that others do not normally consume. You can actually fry banana peels into chips that resemble potatoes. You can consume broccoli leaves, even the stalk, as you would kale. As for meat, go for nose-to-tail recipes, making use of offal and other less popular cuts. They are just as flavorful, even more, than the usual cuts.

✓ When you have a good meal plan, you now have the confidence and strategy to buy in bulk. This will save you some cash. Break bulk purchases into portions, and store properly so you have enough food for a while, and at a lower price. It will be unavoidable to have leftovers, but if you know how to handle and store them properly, this will not be a problem. Invest in some good reusable storage containers and practice the first-in-first-out policy, and you will have a sustainable food supply at home.

✓ If you still have some leftovers or food stocks that you can do nothing about, be charitable and share them. You can share cooked food with your neighbor or co-workers, and you can also donate to food banks or soup kitchens. It's the classic two-birds-one-stone scenario, where you get rid of some stock while feeding people who need it.

✓ My last easy tip is learning to cook and preserve food. I'm not asking you to prepare a five-course meal that Chef Gordon Ramsay would like, just basic meals to feed yourself without making yourself or other people who eat it sick. Meal planning and cooking go hand-in-hand, so you only buy what you are willing to work with on a daily or weekly basis.

✓ Cooked meals generally last longer than raw food because they are heated. This kills off bad microorganisms, as long it is stored properly. You can also portion sizes enough for a meal, so you will not have to thaw out a whole batch, remove a portion, and refreeze. This causes spoilage and degradation of food quality. Also, if you know how to preserve food, you will have snacks or ingredients that last a very long time. The purpose of this book is to show you one particular way of preserving food, dehydration.

PRUNE UP AND DRY UP

Food drying is the oldest of all food preservation techniques. It may require a delicate touch, some science, and a bit of equipment, but once you understand the basic principles, it's a fine skill to have. So, what exactly are you getting?

✓ It's applicable to a lot of food items, and you can extend shelf life significantly. This means years for some items, if you are successful in your endeavors. With a long enough shelf life, you can keep food in storage and not throw it out.

✓ Dried food retains most of its nutrient content, which is great since it makes nutritious food last longer. It gets better, since dried food is more nutrient-dense than fresh. We are removing most of the water content of the food, which lessens the mass, yielding the same nutritional value as less food.

✓ As the nutrients get concentrated, so do the dried food's health benefits. You can get more vitamins, enzymes, and antioxidants with comparatively less food. The antioxidants from dried fruits and vegetables help in fighting cancer, and the fiber aids in smooth bowel movements. The enzymes from dry cured meats help improve the digestive system's environment allowing more efficient digestion, as well as toxin filtration.

✓ However, vitamins A, B, and C may be reduced or destroyed when dehydrating as these vitamins are water-soluble and are mixed with the water content. Dry curing, a type of dehydration process used on meat, usually involves adding quite a bit of salt to keep it from spoiling. So, keep this in mind when incorporating dried food into your diet.

✓ With less water and less space, dried food is easy to store and transport. A pound of meat or fruit will end up only weighing about half a pound or less, so there is no problem stacking items up in your pantry or fridge.

✓ With less power comes more calories. This is not exactly a good thing if you like to gobble up a lot of food in one sitting. However, during wintertime, or if you want to meet your daily calorie requirement with less food, then it's perfect. This is why jerky is popular among hunters and survivalists, since it only takes a small amount of food to maintain caloric requirements.

✓ Dried fruits yield increased caloric value because of the amount of concentrated sugar in them compared to fresh fruits. Again, it's a double-edged sword. If you are just lying around the house or sitting in an office, an increase in sugar intake may not be a good thing. It can just make you gain weight. However, if you have an active lifestyle, and do a lot of physically strenuous activities, the concentrated sugar content of dried fruits can give you that energy to go stronger and longer.

✓ If your location's climate is conducive to it, you can process your dried food naturally, saving money on electricity, and with a smaller carbon footprint. I'll be talking about drying conditions in later sections of this book.

✓ Another thing that dried food brings to the table is convenience. Imagine coming home after a stressful day, and forgetting to buy something to cook for dinner. You can have your dried food for snacks right there, waiting in your pantry. If you are not in the mood for chewing something though, you can rehydrate dried food, and cook as you would raw. And, it has a more intense flavor.

ANCIENT CIVILIZATIONS AND DRIED FOOD

Dehydration might seem like a dry topic, but its history goes a long way back, and might even be as old as humankind. The first type of food that was dried was meat, during prehistoric times. As soon as our species discovered fire, we immediately applied it to meat. Cooking and smoking slabs of wildebeest, or whatever our ancestors managed to catch, added flavor and delayed spoilage.

Drying was the primary way to keep food without it spoiling too quickly. Refrigeration was only available roughly before 1000 BC, and even then, it was only available to those within and near subtropic and colder regions of the globe. Almost all of the early civilizations had some sort of dried food, or at least a dried ingredient.

Even if they were in different regions, and even if they had access to ice, drying food was still part of the culture. Starting off in the Far East, the ancient Japanese and Chinese people were known to lay out fish and meat under the sun to preserve them.

The common folk enjoyed dried fish or squid, while the more opulent citizens prized dried scallops and abalone, which are still expensive to this day. Mongolians carried a dried milk product called *aaruul* as a snack, together with some dried meat, as they rode their powerful horses.

The Mesopotamians salt-cured their meat and fish first, and then dried it under the hot Arabian sun before storing it in clay jars. The nearby Ottomans and Persians wrapped fruits, particularly dates and apricots, in leaves and buried them under the sand, which absorbed the moisture and concentrated the sugar content. The Africans knew all about drying since they were used to the harsh sun, but the Egyptians took it further and dehydrated the corpses of pharaohs and noblemen.

Speaking of Europeans, the Ancient Greeks and Romans salt-cured their meats, using mined salt that had some traces of nitrate. This turned the muscles in the meat a really tempting red color. This is why the Italians now have awesome-looking cold cuts like prosciutto and pancetta. They also dried grapes and peas for easy rehydration during the off-season. So, you can thank them for those pea snacks and raisins.

Medieval Europe also valued dried goods as staple ingredients. Aside from getting some dried products by trading with or invading other areas around the Mediterranean Sea, they also dried their own. Famously, England has a rather cold and rainy climate, so the sun is quite hard to come by. So, they dried their food by fire, baking and smoking the products to remove moisture. Fish and meat were salt cured first, and then dried, while whole grains were dried on trays. Dried food is made for easy transport during travel.

Across the Atlantic Ocean, we arrive in the Americas. To the south first was the great Inca Empire, which spanned the western coast of South America. Such a large area meant more than one climate. In the tropical areas, salted and dried fish, seaweed, and llama meat, were the typical diet. Preserving numerous types of potato and tuberous crops sustained the Incans over the lean season. Inhabitants of areas with subtropical climates and higher elevations made *chuño* which can be bought to this day.

Chuño are potatoes which have been exposed to cold Peruvian night mountain air. The potatoes are mashed, pressed, and then dried in the warm sun several times. Although they resemble small rocks, *chuño* are extremely light, and can be stored for several months or even years.

Chuño often become part of a meal, as they can be thrown right into the stew pot.

Going up north a bit, we have the mighty Mayan and Aztec civilizations, whose diet prioritized five major crops: maize, beans, chili peppers, squash, and cacao-- maize or corn and cacao, were considered the most important. These civilizations used drying to process ingredients, rather than the final product. The nixtamalization of maize involves drying the kernels on the cob, removing them from the cob, and then cooking and soaking them in limewater.

This alkaline solution softens the cell walls within the kernels, and even increases maize's nutritional value. The nixtamal maize can't be cooked as is, or dried once again, but it is ground into fine powder to make *masa harina*. The same goes for cacao beans, which are fermented first and then dried and ground to get cocoa powder. Bitter hot cocoa was drunk with a sprinkling of crushed dried chili pepper.

Finally, to North America. When the first settlers came, they were taught how to preserve through smoking and sun drying by the Native Americans. The settlers found that the Native Americans were drying bison meat, fish, herbs, and vegetables for both food and medicine.

In the centuries and millennia that followed, we still dry our food, even with the advancements in food technology. There is a constant need to make food last longer, as well as to increase its availability and convenience. We have also developed new ways to dry food like turning dehydrators into countertop appliances, so that people who do not experience an ideal drying climate can dehydrate food items right inside their homes.

On an industrial scale, we have developed freeze drying, which effectively makes dried food retain its original qualities when rehydrated. Dehydration led to the some of the world's greatest innovations in food and medicine, like dry yeast, vitamin and vaccines, coffee granules, astronaut and military food, dried pasta, instant noodles, bouillon cubes, and powdered milk.

Dehydration Methods, Tools & Accessories You Will Need, and Tips

Let's now move to how exactly you will dehydrate your food. There are actually several options available to you, and I will go through each one. Each method has its own Tools & Accessories You Will Need and safety precautions. Read each method and figure out what is right for you. I have tried most of these, so I have my own preferences, but I can tell you that there is no one method to rule them all. Each has its own use and pairs well with certain food items.

Sun Drying Solar dehydrators

Sun-drying is the most traditional and simplest of all dehydration methods. However, it comes with specific requirements that should match the climate where you are working.

How to Sun Dry?

As the name suggests, it's as simple as exposing the food item to the heat of the sun. This is how our ancestors dried their food, but, quite frankly, they had a different concept of what was sanitary. After years of research and trial-and-error, it's now a basic ground rule to not sun dry food items if your area is too humid and the ambient temperature, while under the sun, never goes above 85°F. Basically, the US Southwest is the ideal place for sun drying.

Under those conditions, a typical piece of food will take about three to four days to completely dry, depending on how it was cut and the original moisture content. Because of this, it would be best to use fruits with high acid and sugar content as these protect the food from bacteria, mold, and other microorganisms that may spoil the food during the drying time. You can also cure food items beforehand with salt, sugar, or both, as you would with meat, so that microorganisms will not grow on the surface.

TOOLS & ACCESSORIES YOU WILL NEED

You will only need simple equipment to sun dry. A clean table or surface can serve as your drying bed. You will also need several cooling racks for the food, to allow liquid to drip from the bottom and for air to circulate under it. You can also make your own drying racks using a sheet of stainless-steel wire mesh wire attached to wooden frames. Just choose a mesh size that can accommodate the food that you are trying to dry.

For drying fish, you can tie two pieces of fish together by the tail and wedge them on a thick dowel or stick, then place the stick on a high brace or stand. You can also make a drying line like a conventional clothesline, to hang both fish and meat. This is how some people in Asia and Europe dry fish.

For added protection, I also use a separate wire mesh, net, or polyethylene tent to serve as a food drying cover. This allows the sunlight through while keeping bugs and windblown debris out.

You can also construct a solar dehydrator, which is just a dedicated box for sun drying. Some solar dehydrator plans show constructing a trapezoidal box or simply a box tilted diagonally using a window frame, or a slide in a piece of glass for the cover. This will keep bugs and debris out, while still allowing the rays of the sun through. Venting holes are cut along the bottom and top of the container, so cold air can flow in from the bottom and hot air can flow out of the top. You can also line the inside with black-painted metal sheets to absorb more heat, while others use aluminum foil or glass to provide reflective heat.

You can also find a more complex solar dehydrator design wherein they use a shallow yet wide box with a glass panel where air can flow in and heat up. The structure is inclined so that hot air flows upward, where it leads to a box, where the racks of food are placed. This design allows the use of hot air without exposing the food directly to the sun. Either way, as long as you get the concept of using hot flowing air to dry the food, you can design and construct your own solar dehydrator with the Tools & Accessories You Will Need and materials available to you. It will be a fun project.

TIPS AND SAFETY

✓ Like I said earlier, sun drying is best used for highly acidic and sweet fruits. Molds and other stuff can quickly grow on vegetables before they completely dry up.

✓ If you are sun drying meat, I suggest salt curing it first, and trimming off all of the fat. The salt will kill off any harmful bacteria that may grow on the meat. Exposing fat to sunlight causes some oils to go rancid. You can also use an indirect solar dehydrator that only uses air heated by the sun so the fat will not go rancid.

✓ Raise the drying racks by an inch or two off of the drying beds to get good air circulation underneath, and so the food items are not touching any liquid that may have seeped out of them.

✓ Cut your fruits into wide yet thin shapes to expose as much surface area to the sun and to dry faster.

✓ Always lay down food pieces in a single layer. It's all right if they are touching, as long they are not overlapping or on top of each other. This is to maximize exposure to the sun and to avoid any moist environments that will form in between pieces that overlap.

✓ Dry food lasts a long time, and its surface is not conducive to bacterial growth. However, there is a window of opportunity between raw food to dried food where bacteria and other microorganisms can flourish. A handy principle when checking your dried food is "if in doubt, throw it out." This will apply to all types of food, and all drying methods. Inspect for any mold growth. If it's hairy and dark in color, throw that piece out, or cut it off before it infects the rest of your batch.

Air Drying

It may be plain logic that heat allows water to evaporate, however, there is another school of thought on the subject. You can actually dry food using cool dry air. I actually prefer this as it does not use heat, thus, not cooking the food into dryness. It simply removes the water.

How to Air Dry?

This is just like sun drying, except you keep out the sun. You just need a well-ventilated area with low humidity. You can actually do this outside, and inside the house as well. The key thing happening here is osmosis. Your food has moisture in it, giving it a high water potential, while air with low humidity has less water in it, with low water potential.

The osmosis process is the movement of solvent, in this case water, from where there is to where there isn't in order to achieve balance. Since in air drying, we are constantly exposing the surface of the food to dry air, the air absorbs the moisture from the food. The process stops when the air has high humidity and can't absorb more moisture. That is why good airflow is necessary so that you will always have fresh. dry air.

TOOLS & ACCESSORIES YOU WILL NEED

First and foremost, you have to look for an area where you can air dry. It can be anywhere with good airflow and where you won't mind having food drying. Keep in mind though that the immediate area where you are drying your food will smell like the food that you are drying. Some people hang their dried goods around the kitchen. That way, the smell will not be out of place, and might even add to the ambiance. You can also use an unused attic or shed for this, which can be ventilated with a fan.

If you want something smaller, or don't like the idea of hanging dead fish around the house, you can construct a dry box. You can use a small dedicated fridge for this, or a ventilated shed. Put an electric dehumidifier inside and you are golden.

Another way to air dry is by attaching food along a length of string and hanging it in your house, which works for garlic, chilis, corn, herbs, and even fish. You will need a good string that is not fibrous, so I suggest butcher's twine and a large needle in the correct size. You can actually just tie some food items with a knot on the twine, but I find it easier just to just pass the needle and twine through the food.

A wooden frame with a wire mesh can also hold the food and provides better air circulation than on a string since each piece of food will have its own space. It will take a larger area, though.

For both string or wire mesh air drying, I suggest crafting a covering that does not impede air flow. Air drying can take anywhere between three days to two weeks depending on the size and shape of what you are drying. A cover will keep out dust that can fall onto your food during that time. For strings, I cut out round cardboard and pass the string through the middle of it like a makeshift roof. For a whole tray of food, I just place a baking tray over it with a few inches of space.

I have actually tried to air dry meat and fruits inside the fridge. That way, I don't have to worry about dust getting on my food. The smell from the food that I'm drying does affect the butter. This can be a good or bad thing depending on your taste or your use for the butter.

Another neat trick that I learned from Alton Brown is placing the items that you are going to dry on the ridges of cellulose furnace filters-- brand new, clean, and with the grates removed, please. Then you just have to stack them up on top of each other and cover with another furnace filter, and secure them on a box fan with bungee cords. Let the fan run overnight or for two days, and you have perfectly dried goods. This works well with jerky, fruits, and herbs. If you are drying something with a lot of moisture using this method, like fruits, sandwich the food between two dehydrator liners to keep them in place and to not fully soak the furnace filters.

TIPS AND SAFETY

✓ Remember that dark and hairy molds are bad. If it's white and powdery though, some will consider that a good thing, particularly for meat, since that indicates a penicillium white mold. This is what penicillin is made from, and keeps your product clean and, as an antibiotic, prevents the growth of harmful molds and bacteria.

Rawfully Tempting

✓ If you are trying to dry a large and thick piece of meat or whole fruits, you can also look into getting a water activity meter to make sure that the food is dry enough for your liking.

✓ Let everyone in the house know that you are drying something in a particular room. You wouldn't want someone accidentally opening the shower in the spare bathroom you are using to bump into your trays.

✓ If you want to dry in your fridge, make sure that your fridge is completely dry. There should never be any open or exposed food or drinks in it. It's best to isolate a portion of your fridge for drying to avoid accidentally spilling something onto your food. I like the fridge because the temperature slows down bacterial growth, and it also has good air flow.

✓ If you are drying outdoors, do check on your food every hour or so, and bring it inside during the night. I would rather delay the drying process by bringing the food in, instead of letting some wild animal get to it. The aroma of dried food gets quite intense, so it will definitely attract wildlife.

Oven and Microwave Drying

This is a simple method of drying, making use of something you already have at home. Your oven is actually like a dehydrator, particularly if it's a convection oven, since it has a fan to blow the hot air around. Though ovens operate at a higher temperature, we can work around that.

HOW TO USE AN OVEN OR MICROWAVE FOR DRYING?

Just arrange your food on a tray, place it in the oven, set it to the lowest possible level, and keep it there until totally dried. Simple enough, right? This is very accessible if it's your first time, and you already have an oven. If you don't have an oven, will I suggest you get one just for dehydrating food? No, absolutely not. Only use this method if you are drying something quick like herbs, or maybe some fruit leather.

The problem is, this is a resource-exhaustive process. If you own an ordinary electric oven, you are looking at a drying time of two to three days for anything thicker than fruit leather or herbs, and that will definitely rack up your electricity bill. So, reserve this method for trying out a very small batch as a test, or for dried herbs.

You may ask, can a microwave oven dry things faster? Based on my experience, my answer is both a yes and a no.

Yes, the microwave can heat up and evaporate moisture rather quickly. No, the final product does not taste very good. A microwave works by bombarding the food with electromagnetic radiation at a very small frequency that it agitates liquid molecules, causing it to heat up. So, essentially, it's boiling the food from the inside. If you try to dehydrate meat or fruits in a microwave, it becomes extremely tough and tastes like over-boiled food. Stick to herbs when drying in the microwave, and only in small quantities.

TOOLS & ACCESSORIES YOU WILL NEED

An electric convection oven is the best option under this category, since it provides the necessary amount of heat, plus it has a fan to distribute that heat. You can also use an air fryer, since it's just a smaller convection oven. However, air fryers will not function with the food basket ajar, which is essential since we need to keep the fan on, and an opening for the moisture to vent out. So, it will take a long time for an air fryer to dry food, and you can only do a small amount at a time.

A regular electric oven will work, but takes a relatively long time to finish drying. At least you can process a whole lot more at a time than in an air fryer. As I mentioned, you will have the best dehydrating result with a microwave if you just use it for herbs. Otherwise, there are a lot of things a microwave can do better than dehydration.

Other Tools & Accessories You Will Need you need under this category are trays. They are best used for fruit leathers or whole fruits, since they are quite juicy and will release quite a lot of juice. These juices will just stain your oven if you don't use a tray. Silicone mats are also nice when making fruit leather, since these will make it easy to peel off. If you are drying jerky fish or other meat products, just place it directly on the oven racks, or a cooling rack if the pieces are small and can fall through an oven rack. Using these exposes more surface area of the food pieces to the warm air from your oven.

TIPS AND SAFETY

✓ I purposely did not suggest using gas ovens for drying, since I will not advise keeping a gas oven running for over 12 hours unattended. Your gas connections might be very secure, but I would rather err on the side of caution and safety, than risk it over a couple of dried strawberries. If you are just using a gas oven to dry herbs or fruit leather, then go ahead, and check on it every 30 minutes or so.

✓ When using a convection oven, make a ping pong-sized ball of aluminum foil, and wedge it between the trigger switch and door of your oven. This will keep the oven running, as well as providing a small opening for the warm, moisture-laden air from within to escape, drying your food faster.

✓ Do not use the plastic dehydrator liners in your oven since they are designed for relatively low temperatures. An oven's temperature output is like a wave, going up and down a few degrees from the set temperature, so it might go too high and melt the plastic. However, silicone dehydrator liners are safe to use.

✓ For a more even drying, only occupy the middle three or four rack levels of your oven. Filling up all of the racks with food will take a longer drying time, with the ones right in front of the fan going exponentially quicker than the rest.

✓ Use an oven thermometer to get a more accurate reading of your oven's lowest temperature range. We are aiming for a temperature of 140°F or lower. Anything more than that and you are essentially baking the food. If your oven's lowest operating temperature is over 140°F, I suggest that you save on electricity and just air dry or sun dry. You can use the oven racks for them, too.

✓ A nice little trick to turn your oven into a dehydrator is to buy a ceramic heat bulb and place it in the oven to provide heat. Yup, these are the special light bulbs used to warm up reptiles in terrariums during winter. Add a small handheld portable fan in there, and a ball of aluminum foil to prop the oven door open by about two inches for good air circulation. This is a good cheap option for thicker pieces of fruit and vegetables.

Electric Dehydrators

This is the standard equipment people get for home dehydration. It's a bit of an investment, but if you dry food every other week or so, I think it's worth it.

HOW TO USE AN ELECTRIC DEHYDRATOR?

Think of an electric dehydrator as a convection oven that operates at a lower temperature, and eats up less energy. It also has adjustable temperatures, with some manufacturers indicating the corresponding food item per temperature level. So, simply arrange food pieces onto the racks provided, place it in your dehydrator, set the temperature, and let it run. It might take several hours or a whole day for food to dry, but since it operates on electricity, and consumes less energy, there is little to no problem to keep it running that long. Electric dehydrators are designed to handle almost all types of items that can be dried, so although it only has one function (to dehydrate), it's still quite useful.

TOOLS & ACCESSORIES YOU WILL NEED

Heater and fan placement can be at the bottom or at the side, separating electric dehydrators into two major types. Vertical dehydrators are usually cheaper than the horizon39tal ones, and you can buy additional racks and stack them higher. However, vertical dehydrators are prone to uneven drying, since the air loses its warmth as it goes up the layers. Adding more racks compounds this problem, making overall drying time longer, and forcing you to swap rack placements as you dry.

Horizontal dehydrators, on the other hand, dry all racks evenly, since the heat source and fan blow from the side, passing through each layer at the same time. This mechanic also prevents the intermingling of flavors, in case you are drying different types of food together. Horizontal dehydrators are quite expensive though, and you are limited in capacity. If you want to dry more food per batch, then you will have to buy additional dehydrators.

Since they produce a lower temperature, some dehydrators are made out of food grade plastic, which can either be a good or bad thing. It's good since it will be cheaper if made out of plastic, which is why most vertical dehydrators are affordable compared to horizontal ones. Keep in mind that even if the plastic can handle the relatively lower heat, there is still heat that can warp the plastic. This gives the dehydrators with plastic construction a relatively shorter life span than those constructed like an oven.

Which one is better? Well, it depends, really. If you are just starting out, and will probably dry a batch every other week, or on a monthly basis, then you can get a vertical dehydrator, which ranges from $40 to $80 depending on size. If you are planning to dry a batch every week or more frequently, I suggest saving up and getting a large horizontal dehydrator, which ranges from $70 to $800 depending on the size. I feel like when you get the ones priced at $800 or more (horizontal dehydrator), you might as well make a living out of dried food.

Other equipment that you might need are silicone dehydrator liners. Some of the racks that come with the dehydrators have wide grates that pieces of food might fall through, so a liner with smaller mesh size is needed.

✓ Dehydrators are countertop appliances, so choose one that can fit your available space. A small horizontal dehydrator is close to the size of a medium microwave oven.

✓ A working dehydrator will give off some humidity, and lots of aroma. So, place it somewhere near the stove or a window.

✓ Your dehydrator should have good heat control. As I have mentioned, some just have settings indicated by the type of food, but I think it will be better if you can set the dehydrator to the temperature that you like, so you may shorten or extend the drying time. Drying time determines the texture of your final product. A good range is about 80°F to 160°F, which covers most types of food.

✓ Common vertical dehydrators have a fan and heat source at the center bottom of the dehydrator, so look for a circular one, to get as much warm air as possible. Rectangular vertical dehydrators with the same heat source placement will only dry the immediate area around the source, leaving the corners cool.

✓ Some dehydrators come with liners, but in case the one you bought doesn't have any, I suggest buying liners in

48

the same number as your racks. It makes for easier loading, and you will not have to cut your recipe in case you run out of liners.

✓ Choose silicone liners over plastic ones as the plastic tends to warp after several uses. Silicone lasts longer, is flexible, and can be used in your oven too.

✓ A silicone mat and tray combination is great for drying paste or liquid products. Have some of those handy as well. They also work in your oven, so it's a good all-around tool to have.

✓ When positioning each piece on the rack, it's fine for them to touch, but not to overlap. This makes each piece dry faster and more evenly.

✓ In a pinch, you may use parchment paper as a liner. However, do not use plastic wrap, as it does not allow ventilation, leaving your food pieces dry on the top and wet at the bottom. Also, don't use wax paper. The heat is enough to melt the wax off your paper and transfer it to your food. A cooling rack or a clean metal wire mesh will work, also.

Freeze Drying

Freeze drying is a dehydration technique that is more often done in an industrial setting. It lasts longer compared to other dried food, even without refrigeration. This is why this is the preferred way to preserve food for military personnel on the frontlines, and astronauts in space.

HOW TO FREEZE DRY?

The process for freeze drying is actually quite complex. First, the temperature is brought down to about -112°F. Once there, the pressure is also brought down while raising the temperature by a few degrees, sublimating the ice crystals. This cycle is repeated again, but this time, the temperature is raised to 32°F. The second cycle will remove whatever moisture was left from the first freeze drying cycle, leaving a final product with only about 1% to 4% moisture content.

This whole process is simply executed by the press of a button. The machine itself monitors the temperature and pressure, changing the parameters at the very exact moment to get the maximum amount of moisture out.

This is actually how Peruvian *chuño* are made, and manually at that. However, *chuño* requires days of freezing, squeezing, and sun drying, all with the perfect ambient temperatures at different times of the day. So, it's essentially not a replicable process.

TOOLS & ACCESSORIES YOU WILL NEED

Because of the complex process, and the mechanical sophistication needed to do it, freeze drying is mainly done at the industrial level. This is how dry yeast, powdered milk, instant noodles, and even medicines are manufactured.

If, however, you have $2,600 to $5,000 to spare, then you can buy your own home freeze dryer. At that price range, the capacity ranges from four to 35 lbs. of food. It will be like operating an electric dehydrator. Simply arrange your prepared food pieces on the trays, place it in the freeze dryer, lock it up, and turn it on.

TIPS AND SAFETY

✓ Read your freeze dryer's manual. This equipment has many delicate parts, so maintain it in good condition.

✓ Opaque Mylar® bags sealed with a vacuum sealer are the essential storage container for freeze dried food. These keep out humidity, light, and oxygen.

✓ Trim off as much fat or remove as much oil from food that you are going to freeze dry, as these do not dry well. Always look for lean proteins.

Dry Curing

This isn't necessarily a dehydrating technique, but it does go well with dehydration. Dry curing is preparing the food item, mainly meat, by curing it with some salt first before drying. The salt kills off bacteria and prevents further growth, giving a larger margin of error during the drying process. Dry curing also offers the opportunity to dry at a slower rate and at a relatively higher humidity, fermenting the product and imparting a unique flavor.

HOW TO DRY CURE?

For dry curing, the piece of food can be kept whole. Wipe it down with some paper towels, which produces a slightly dry and sticky surface. Then, add salt. There are two main ways to do this. The first is the salt box method, wherein you find a container for the food you are going to dry. Sprinkle about an inch layer of salt at the bottom of the container. Gently place the food in the container, and bury it with more salt. Do try to look for a container that will only leave about an inch of space all around to save on salt. After a few days, depending on the size of the piece (a few hours for fish), excavate the food, give it a rinse, and dry it by sun drying, air drying, or with an electric dehydrator.

The other way to cure is equilibrium curing. This is done by weighing the piece of meat you are going to dry, then rubbing a precisely measured amount of salt on it. The salt measurement is usually 2% to 4% of the raw weight of the meat, depending on the shape and recipe being followed. Place it in a zip-lock bag, sealing with the air removed. Place it in the fridge and leave it for a week or three. Since the salt is precisely measured, there is no risk of oversalting. You just then have to dry it by air drying, sun drying, or with an electric dehydrator.

TOOLS & ACCESSORIES YOU WILL NEED

For the preparation side of the salt box method, you will need containers that fit the particular piece of food that you are drying. It will just be in contact with salt and meat juices, so it's okay to do it in plastic containers, like an old ice cream tub. For equilibrium curing, you just need some zip-lock bags which fits the piece of meat.

For the drying phase, you can use the same equipment for air drying, sun drying, and an electric dehydrator. If you are using a fridge that you retrofitted into a dry box, you can take this opportunity and add a bit of equipment. You can get a plug-in thermostat, electric dehumidifier, and an electric humidifier.

Set the thermostat to a temperature range of 55°F to 60°F, and a humidity range of 70% to 80%. In that sweet spot, you can prolong the drying to about three months, and actually ferment the meat further. It may grow some penicillium white mold, develop some funk, and a more intense taste. This is the distinct flavor of salami, pepperoni, and prosciutto. Since we are using a fridge as a dry box, it's relatively easy to clean and disinfect.

You can cut back on the electric humidifier and dehumidifier and get a hygrometer and a small fan. Simply place the hygrometer's probe inside the fridge and the fan to keep the air moving. In case the humidity goes down, place a bowl of water or a wet rolled towel in front of the fan to get the humidity up. If it gets too high, just remove the bowl or wet towel.

You can get a water activity meter, which you can also use for other drying techniques. This tool measures the amount of moisture still in the piece of food that you are drying. It's quite handy for larger cuts of meat, and even thick fruit slices.

TIPS AND SAFETY

✓ This is quite a tricky process with great rewards, and potentially a big failure rate. So, more than ever, please practice the mantra of "if in doubt, throw it out." Cured and fermented meats might have a bit of funk on them, but when it goes off the rail, you will definitely know from the aroma.

✓ If you are using your main kitchen fridge for drying, keep the food that you are drying in an isolated spot. Make sure that there are no other open containers of food or drinks in the fridge. They will increase the moisture in the fridge's atmosphere.

✓ Always have fresh gloves handy. Do not touch the meat with your bare hands while curing. Even when clean, you can drop some dead skin cells or a bit of grime that can become an entry point for bacteria and mold. So, always play it safe and wear gloves.

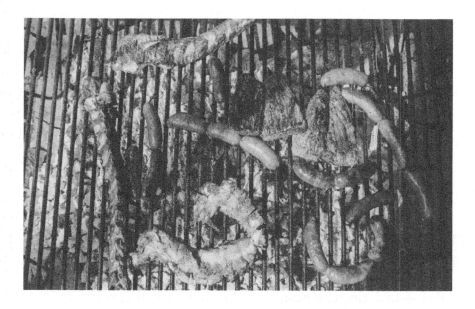

✓ When curing meat, particularly pork, remember that fat is flavor. It also helps with protecting the muscles, making it dry slower and ferment better. A caveat to this tip though, is that fat and sun do not mix. So, when drying a piece of fatty meat, go with an electric dehydrator, or go with the air-drying route.

✓ I have mentioned salt percentages, which should always be properly measured as the recipe suggests. However, you are not limited to just salt. You may also use soy sauce or salt seasoning. You will just have to calculate the actual amount of salt in the mixture, and then the amount of said mixture that will correspond to the salt content needed. As long as you have the salt content correct, you can also mix in some sugar and spices.

✓ Aside from the salt content, you should also precisely measure out the amount of curing salt, also known as Prague powder #2 or pink salt, which should never be confused with the Himalayan pink salt. This is a specially formulated salt, with nitrite and nitrate mixed in, which kills bacteria more effectively, but can cause an upset stomach when it's eaten at large amounts. That is why it's usually mixed in with regular salt, at around 1.5% or less of the meat's wet weight. The mixture of nitrite and nitrate have the added bonus of keeping the muscle fibers naturally red, and enticing.

Smoking

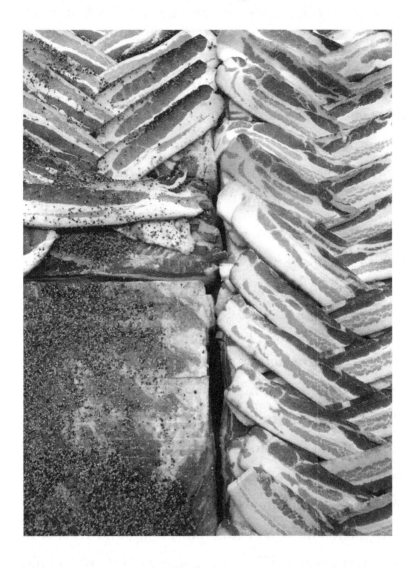

There are two ways to smoke food. Each has its merits, and best uses for different types of food. Smoking is also not limited to meat, as you can smoke fish, shellfish, herbs, and vegetables.

How to Smoke?

Smoking is actually both similar to, and an additional treatment to, salt curing. Aside from adding some great flavor, the smoke also lowers the pH of the food surface, which kills off harmful bacteria and inhibits further growth. The smoke may penetrate the food, but its preservative properties, not so much. That is why in some cases, salt curing comes first.

Cold smoking, as the name suggests, is the application of smoke to food without the addition of heat. This is done using a heat source to generate smoke. The smoke is directed or pumped toward the food. In some cases, like in cold smoking sausage, salt curing may be necessary to prevent bacterial growth.

Hot smoking, on the other hand, applies smoke to the food surface, and at the same time, heats up the food, killing off any bacteria.

Tools & Accessories You Will Need

You will, of course, need a smoker. It can be bought or made, but in general, there are two types: horizontal or vertical. Because of the placement of the firebox, a vertical smoker is perfect for hot smoking. You may lower the temperature as much as you can, but the smoker still heats up. Because of the heat it generates, a vertical smoker dries more effectively.

The horizontal smoker can both cold smoke and hot smoke because of the placement of the firebox. You can also use it as a dryer. But since a horizontal smoker has no fan, it will dry only the food closest to the firebox quickest.

TIPS AND SAFETY

✓ When there is smoke, there is usually fire, so be careful. Always have a fire extinguisher ready nearby, and have the necessary Tools & Accessories You Will Need at hand. Have fireproof gloves, tongs, a shovel and a stoker, depending on the size of your smoker.

✓ If you have an electric smoker, make sure that the plug and connections stay dry. You are, of course, smoking outdoors, so there will always be risks. If you have guests, make sure that they stay clear of electrical cords and the smoker itself.

✓ Make sure to use seasoned wood, or proper smoker pellets. Fresh or "green" wood make for dense smoke, which gives a nasty, sooty taste to your food if it is exposed for a long duration. Billowy smoke is natural when adding new wood to a fire, but it will only last a minute or two before clearing up to the ideal blue wispy smoke. Using fresh wood can also make it difficult to manage a fire.

✓ When smoking meat or other proteins, be it for drying or just general barbecue smoking, place your meat in the fridge the night before, uncovered. This will dry the surface just enough to get a sticky "pellicle", or film, and will allow the smoke to stick better. The better the smoke adhesion, the better the flavor.

✓ Position your food with about half an inch of space between each piece so that the smoke has space to flow through and completely cover the surface.

Dehydrofreezing

Dehydrofreezing is a relatively new concept. It's a combination of drying and freezing processes, but it is not similar to freeze drying.

HOW TO DEHYDROFREEZE?

We actually discussed the processes needed to dehydrofreeze in the previous sections. What you need to do first is to dry your food using any method that you like. However, you are going to stop when you have a 50% to 60% moisture loss. Then, the food is immediately transferred into the freezer to freeze solid. Food items that are dehydrofrozen are not necessarily fit for immediate consumption.

Dehydrofreezing is designed for eventual rehydration. The food pieces that underwent dehydrofreezing have had their flavor concentrated from the partial dehydration and preserved through freezing, giving them a better flavor when rehydrated. Also, since they were not fully dehydrated, there was no cell collapse. The rehydrated food comes out very close to its original state when rehydrated. It rehydrates faster too.

TOOLS & ACCESSORIES YOU WILL NEED

For the dehydrating portion of the process, you will need the same Tools & Accessories You Will Need that you will use for the dehydrating method of your choice. Unless you are really adept at estimating the water loss of your food, you will need a water activity meter to accurately determine when you are in the sweet spot of 50% moisture loss.

For the freezing, you will need a freezer, of course, and some baking trays. You will need to have ample space in your freezer to fit the trays, containing the evenly spaced food. This is actually similar to the individual quick freezing (IQF) method, which freezes food pieces quickly, avoiding freezer burn (ice crystals forming on the surface). Once frozen, you may transfer the food pieces to a container or freezer-friendly zip-lock bags.

Tips and Safety

✓ As with everything else, to make things go faster, cut your food into small or thin pieces, particularly during the freezing phase. We do not want the pieces to shrivel up and squeeze out more moisture. This causes cell collapse and freezer burn, which makes a mushy, unappetizing texture upon rehydration. So, speed is key here.

✓ Since we want speed, it's best to use metallic baking trays when freezing, like aluminum, stainless steel, or carbon steel. The metals, being conductors, absorb the heat from the food faster and release the heat in the cold freezer environment just as fast.

✓ When freezing on the tray, spread out the food pieces to form just one layer, maximizing the surface area of the tray for faster freezing time. You can also freeze the trays beforehand. And, after spreading out the food pieces on one tray, you can place another ice-cold tray on top to decrease the heat in a matter of seconds.

✓ Carefully measure the moisture loss of your food during the dehydration phase, as you will not want the cells to collapse. In case you accidentally exceed the target moisture loss, don't worry and keep drying. You can still fully dehydrate it as you normally would. Just try again next time.

✓ Keep in mind that products of dehydrofreezing are suited for rehydration. So, treat the raw counterparts of those items as you normally would. You may eat fruits raw, but for meat, and some of the vegetables, you will have to cook them first before consuming.

GENERAL TIPS

Here are some general tips for preparing your food for drying, plus some general safety tips.

✓ When drying uncured meat, the U.S. Department of Agriculture (USDA) specifies that the meat should first be cooked. Poultry should first be cooked to a temperature of 165°F, while whole cuts of other meat should be cooked to 145°F, and then rested for 3 minutes before drying. However, if you are going to freeze dry uncured meat, then you can put it straight into your freeze dryer raw or cooked.

✓ To facilitate faster and even drying, cut your fish into fillets. You can also cut them from the top of the head, all the way to the tail, but don't go through the bottom part of the fish. This way, you can butterfly the fish open, and clean out the innards at the same time.

✓ For fleshy and pulpy fruits and vegetables, cut them as little or as thinly as you can for faster drying. For those with lots of water content, like citrus, tomatoes, and berries, keep them whole or just halved, since they will give off a lot of moisture and shrivel up significantly.

✓ For items that may slip through dehydrator racks, like grains and pastes, use silicone mats or metal trays. The mats are flexible, making it easy to peel off fruit leathers, while metal trays become hot and quickly dry off grains.

✓ Always form a single layer when drying your food for even drying. Spread it out evenly on racks or trays. Don't mound it up. It's better to dry single-layered trays twice or thrice rather than cramming everything and forcing your dehydrator to dry them for a longer time.

✓ Regarding the pandemic and drying, hygiene is key. Keep in mind that sometimes items are not cooked to kill bacteria but rather held in the "zone" for a bit of time. It's therefore imperative not to introduce bacteria to lessen the risks. Keep a stock of surgical gloves.

✓ To further reduce the risk of contamination to zero, you can cure the food before drying. You can use salt and pink salt for meats. For fruits and vegetables, major manufacturers use potassium metabisulfite, also known as

"Campden tablets", to kill any bacteria. Campden tablets are also used to preserve wines and sanitize wine-making equipment. The tablets are edible and safe to use in small amounts. However, they can lead to a coughing fit if you accidentally take a whiff from the container. The usual dilution is about 1/16 teaspoon, or a tablet per gallon, or 8 lbs. of fruit. A little goes a long way, as a one-pound bag of Campden tablets can last a year or two. Keep them in a dry, airtight container.

✓ Speaking of Campden tablets, you can also dilute a tablet in a gallon of water, and pour some it into a spray bottle. Spray it on your cutting board, drying mats, drying lines, and dehydrator liners to sanitize them for use. You can pour the rest of the cleaning solution into a large bowl or basin and soak any other equipment that you will be using, like knives, tongs, blender assembly, food processor assembly, bowls, and other utensils.

✓ Electric dehydrators produce uniform products that are finished relatively quickly. However, if you want to cut down on your carbon footprint, go for sun drying or air drying, as these use natural and replenishable energy.

✓ If you are not keen on getting a water activity meter, but eager to start, a cheaper alternative to determining the dryness of the product is by weight loss. Always measure the weight of your product after trimming, but before any processing. Then, weigh it when you think it's nearing the dryness that you want. People usually go for about 40% to 50% weight loss. Fruits and vegetables can even go up to 80% to 90% weight loss.

✓ Since there are many factors to consider, some people just use their experience to determine dryness. As a beginner, you may not have experience in drying but you may have consumed dried food before, so you at least have a basic idea. The brittleness of herbs, the pliability of fruit, or the hardness of meat point to good dryness levels. Take note of the look of dried tomatoes and raisins in the grocery store and compare them to your own products.

✓ As you look for key success indicators, you should also keep an eye out for problems. "If in doubt, throw it out!" Check your finished products for weird, even slimy, textures. Look for mold splotches or strange discolorations. Look for things that should not be there. And be consistent and quick about this. Throw out any infected pieces, or cut out the portion to save your batch. In case you weren't able to discover these issues in time or if you somehow left them to grow and touch other pieces, then the infection will grow further.

✓ I suggest keeping a diary of your journey into the world of dehydration. Take note of the weight of your batches before and after drying. Take note of your curing recipes and final moisture levels. Having a diary allows you to learn from your mistakes and correct them for your next batch. It also helps you with replicating any successful products so you will not make mistakes in the future. Always take notes!

✓ In case you lose a batch, do not just throw it out with the rest of your garbage. These are still organic materials, and you can isolate them and use them for compost later.

We are trying to cut back on food waste here, so we need to make use of any bad products.

✓ In case you have any leftover dried product in the fridge that becomes too hard to snack on, do not throw it out. As long as there is no mold or spoiled spots, these are still good, just overly dried. It's best to use them in soups or stews, even syrups for fruits, to rehydrate them and soften them up.

RECIPES

Fruits

GENERAL FRUIT DEHYDRATION

After the dry curing discussion, you have learned about the preservative properties of salt. However, this may not pair well with the sweet flavor of fruits. Most commercially made dried fruits are mixed with sulfur in the form of potassium metabisulfite.

This is mistaken for vitamin D by bacteria and mold, and they eventually die off. Sulfur also prevents oxidation and the enzymatic process, which causes cut fruits to turn brown. This is perfectly safe, though there are people who have allergic reactions to sulfur, particularly its fumes. Asthmatic people in particular experience adverse reactions to the whole process.

Luckily, we have an acidic option to cure fruit pieces for drying. Citrus hits the three goals we need to cure fruits. It prevents bacteria and mold growth, has antioxidative properties, and stops the enzymatic process. So, here's a general process for dehydrating fruits effectively.

Ingredients:

❖ 32 oz. water

❖ 1 cup fresh lemon juice

❖ Fruit of your choice for dehydrating

Directions:

1. Juice enough lemon to get a full cup of juice. You don't have to worry about the seeds; they can be easily strained out later. Mix the juice with the water until fully integrated.

2. Peel and slice your fruit into small or thin pieces, whichever is applicable to the type of fruit. Place them in

separate bowls per fruit for easy placement on the tray later.

3. Pour the lemon juice mixture into each bowl until the fruit pieces are covered. Do not worry if your lemon juice mixture is not enough for all of the fruit pieces. You will only have to soak them for about 30 seconds. So, you can quickly soak a batch of fruits, strain the juice over a bowl, and use it to soak a different batch. Just repeat until you have everything soaked and ready.

4. Place the fruit pieces into your dehydrator, and process until completely dried. Air drying will take about a whole day or two, while a heated dehydrator will take about 12 hours to 18 hours, depending on the fruit.

5. To check, the fruits should have darkened in color without going brown. The pieces should be able to bend without cracking, and they should feel a bit leathery at room temperature, so better let the pieces cool first. This procedure works well with fibrous and fleshy fruits. Also, check the Storage Section for "conditioning" before setting aside for long-term storage. Oh, and if you are wondering what to do with the leftover lemon juice mixture, you can enjoy it in some fruity cocktails.

If you find regular dried fruits to be a bit boring, then why not ramp up the flavor even more by encasing them in sugar? This forms crystals on the surface of the fruit, giving them a frosty look after drying. This recipe will take about three to four days, but with only 30 minutes of work per day.

Ingredients:

* 5 cups water

* 5 cups sugar

* 1 tbsp. corn syrup

* 1 lb. fruit of your choice for dehydrating

Directions:

1. Set a pot over medium heat, and mix the sugar and water. Boil until the sugar is fully dissolved, and then mix the corn syrup until fully integrated. Lower the heat to maintain a bare simmer.

2. Peel your fruit and slice it into half-inch thick pieces. Transfer finished pieces immediately to the warm syrup to

avoid browning. The amount of syrup should be enough to cover all of the fruit pieces.

3. Maintain a bare simmer for about 20 minutes, and then take it off the heat and let cool to room temperature. Once it cools down, cover the pot, and let it sit on your kitchen counter overnight. Repeat the 20-minute simmering and overnight steeping for three or four times. Replenish with more syrup in case it gets too low, and the fruits are not submerged.

4. For the final simmering, heat the mixture to 235°F to get to the soft ball stage, and let it sit for the last time overnight. Then strain the fruits, and lay them down on the dehydrator racks. Dry until stiff for about 12 to 18 hours. For fleshy fruits, and even for citrus peels, cut into thin strips so you will have less stuff to throw out. For the leftover syrup steeped with fruity flavors, it's great for cocktails, sweetening your tea, or just mixed with soda water for a refreshing drink.

FRUIT LEATHERS

For juicy fruits, let's make use of the natural moisture and pectin to create a malleable paste which can be spread thinly. You will have a uniform-looking dried paste, and will not become wrinkly like whole dried fruits. Fruit leathers are also a great way to mix the flavor of different fruits, or even sneak in some vegetables for the kids.

There is no definite recipe for fruit leathers, as each fruit behaves differently in this recipe. Instead, I will be giving some guidelines on making your own style of fruit leather.

Ingredients:

* 1 lb. fruit of your choice

* Sweetener of your choice, like sugar or honey

* Lemon Juice

Directions:

1. First, peel and roughly chop your fruits then transfer them to a blender. Blend everything until smooth. You can make the paste with a mixture of fruits, or a single type. Since we are using pastes, you can even blend two or more types of fruits separately, and then combine them when drying, giving you a multicolored fruit leather piece.

2. Give the mixture some flavor. Depending on the fruits you are using and its ripeness, see if it needs a bit more sweetness or tartness. If the fruit that you are using browns quickly, like apples, avocado, or blueberries, definitely add a bit of lemon juice. If it gets too tart, balance it out with the addition of sugar or honey. If your fruit paste tastes perfect as it is, use it.

3. Lay down a silicone mat over the dehydrator racks, and evenly spread the fruit paste over it. Dry for about five to six hours until it feels dry to the touch but is still bendable without breaking. You can cut it into strips and

store it, or roll the leather and cut it into 1-inch segments and store that way. If you made a fruit leather sheet with separate types of fruit, roll it up across the columns or divisions. That way, when you cut them into rolled segments, you will get all the flavors in a single strip.

Veggies

GENERAL VEGETABLE DEHYDRATION

Luckily, most vegetables can withstand the rigors of dehydration, so you will not have to cure them with salt or citric acid first. Honestly, curing with salt or citric acid does not mesh with most vegetable flavors. However, some vegetables do require special preparation before drying, mainly starchy vegetables.

For these, you will have to blanch them first. Blanching kills off bacteria and weakens the cell walls in vegetables, making them easier to dry. The hot water also stops the enzymatic process, allowing the dried vegetables to keep their color. Here's a quick procedure on how to blanch and dry vegetables.

Ingredients:

❖ Vegetable of your choice for dehydrating

❖ Water

Directions:

1. Give your vegetables a good rinse and scrub to get rid of any dirt. Set them aside to drain. Have a kitchen spider or strainer ready. Set a pot filled halfway with water over medium heat. Set another bowl nearby, filled halfway with ice water.

2. As the water heats up, peel and cut your vegetables thinly if it's applicable to your choice of vegetables. Once they are cut to sizes, and the water is boiling, drop them into the hot water. Blanching time depends on the type of vegetables you are using, so do not mix different vegetable types when dunking. It's best to only blanch a single type of vegetable at a time.

3. Most vegetables only require four minutes of soaking in hot water, but for harder vegetables like potatoes, corn, or really compacted Brussels sprouts, seven minutes may be necessary. After soaking in hot water, immediately remove the vegetables from the pot using a kitchen spider or strainer, and transfer them to the cold ice water to shock them and stop cooking. Repeat with the rest of your cut vegetables.

4. When you have blanched the rest of the vegetables, drain them, lay them out on your dehydrating rack, and dry as you normally would. Blanching works on a lot of vegetables, but you may skip this step with beets, chili peppers, horseradish, mushrooms, and tomatoes.

DRIED HERBS

Having dried herbs ready is handy for quickly seasoning dishes. They easily add flavor. However, herbs, being the leaves of plants, do go bad rather quickly. Drying them extends their life and flavor, for use in last-minute dinners that impress your guests. This process is great for harder herbs like rosemary, bay, and oregano.

Ingredients:

❖ Fresh herbs of your choice, still on the stem

❖ Water

Directions:

1. Keep your herbs on the stem, and give them a quick rinse just to get rid of any dirt or dust. Pick off any leaves that have browning or blemishes, and throw them out for compost.

2. Set a pot filled halfway with water over medium heat and bring to a boil. Also have a bowl of ice water and a salad spinner nearby. Hold your herbs by the stems, as much as you can hold at a time. Dunk them into the hot water, making sure that the leaves are submerged. It's all right not to soak the stems, and your hand, in the hot water. You are only going to soak them in hot water for five

seconds, and then immediately transfer them to the cold water. Repeat until you have blanched everything.

3. Transfer the herbs into your salad spinner, and spin them to drain off the excess water. Place the relatively dry herbs onto dehydrating racks. You can also tie them up with string, and hang them for air drying. Just make sure to use a dustcover for the air dried ones.

4. You will know that they are well dehydrated when the leaves snap off the stems like potato chips. You can store them whole or rub them between your hands over a flexible cutting board or wax paper. This way, it is easy to separate the leaf flakes from the woody stems easily.

DRIED CHILI

Chilis are in a league of their own when it comes to drying. Maybe because they grow in hot, warm, dry regions, they can be dehydrated without much prior preparation. Chile favor profiles change after drying, so much so that they have specific names.

Ingredients:

❖ Fresh, good quality chilis

Directions:

1. If you have chili plants at home, then you are in luck; otherwise, you will have to go to the grocery store for them. Pick out the best-looking chilis that you can get. They should have bright colors without any blemishes or soft spots, which are signs of spoilage. If you are picking your own chilis from the plant, cut them from the main stem so that you will have an inch or two of stem still attached to the fruit.

2. There are several options for drying. You can use a needle to thread through the stems of the chilis, so they can be hung for air drying. This is the most traditional way, but it can take about three to four weeks for them to dry completely. They may also be dried on dehydrator racks as you normally would.

3. Dry them until they shrivel up and the skin feels waxy yet still malleable. This is so you can keep them whole. You can also dry them until they become brittle, then grind them up into flakes or powder.

Nuts and Grains

Spicy Dry Nuts (and Legume)

Nuts are mainly dried as a snack instead of an ingredient. So, why not make it more exciting by adding flavors to them? This recipe works for different raw nuts, and also for peanuts, which are legumes. Yes, despite having "nut" in its name, a peanut is a legume, and not a nut. Isn't that nuts?

Ingredients:

❖ 1 lb. raw whole nuts of your choice

❖ ½ cup water

❖ ¼ cup soy sauce

❖ 1 tbsp. chili flakes

❖ 1 tsp. ground cumin

❖ 1 tsp. ground coriander seeds

❖ 1 tsp. dried cilantro

❖ Ground black pepper

Directions:

1. Use a large jar that can hold the nuts and the rest of the ingredients. Clean it and dry it well. Place all the ingredients except the nuts in it, and secure the lid. Give the jar a good shake to incorporate everything and to remove clumps of spices.

2. Once fully mixed, open it up and drop in the raw nuts. Secure the lid again, and give it a good shake to remove any air pockets that may stick to the surface of the nuts. Let this sit overnight on the kitchen counter, and away from the sun.

3. Strain the nuts from the liquid, and lay them down in a single layer on a dehydrator rack with a silicone liner. You can also use a metal baking sheet if you run out of liner. Dry until crunchy. As for the leftover marinating liquid, it may be used to season soups. I also use it for boiling noodles, pasta or rice.

DRIED PUMPKIN SEEDS

Aside from nuts, you can also use the same procedure for flavorful seeds snacks. This recipe uses pumpkin seeds, but you can also use squash, watermelon, and sunflower. For this, I'm going for a sweeter flavor profile, so it can be eaten as a dessert, or sprinkled on a bowl of oatmeal or yogurt.

Ingredients:

❖ 1 lb. raw pumpkin seeds

❖ ½ cup water

❖ 2 tbsp. honey

- ❖ 2 tsp. oil (vegetable or almond)

- ❖ 1 tsp. ground cinnamon

- ❖ 1 tsp. grated nutmeg

- ❖ ½ tsp. ground clove

- ❖ Pinch of salt

Directions:

1. Scoop out the pulp of the pumpkin, and sift through it to retain the seeds. The pulp can go into the compost bin, or feed it to your pet for fiber. Place the seeds in a strainer or colander, and rinse well to remove the slippery membranes.

2. Spread the seeds out on a towel to dry a bit. In the meantime, mix the water and a pinch of salt in a large jar. Shake it until fully integrated. Pour the seeds into the jar, close the lid, and shake it to mix and coat. Let it soak overnight.

3. Strain off the seeds, and lay them again on a towel to dry off. Mix the honey, oil, and spices in a bowl, and add the seeds. Mix to fully coat.

4. Spread the seeds on a dehydrator rack with liner, or a metal tray. Dry the seeds until crunchy and flavorful. If properly dried, you can actually eat them without peeling. If you are using sunflower seeds, they will have to crack open to consume, or crack them open before soaking and flavoring.

PASTA

Pasta is a great pantry staple, and can get you out of a lot of emergency meal scenarios. Sure, you can get dried pasta easily from the store, but if you make it yourself, you can customize it to your needs. It makes you appreciate the process of making your own food. It's easy to make, and gives you some kitchen bragging rights, even if just to yourself.

Ingredients:

❖ 1 lb. semolina flour (For classic pasta flavor, use all-purpose flour)

❖ 1 tsp. salt

❖ 3 whole eggs

❖ 1 egg yolk

❖ Water

Directions:

1. Flour is an agricultural product, so there is no exact recipe. It's all about the feeling. On a clean kitchen counter or a large cutting board, pour about ¾ lbs. of the flour into a mound. Make a well in the center.

2. I normally like to use four to five egg yolks, but I can only eat so many egg white omelets, so three whole eggs and an additional egg yolk will do. Crack the eggs one at a time in a small bowl or ramekin before depositing them into the flour well. This is to avoid ruining the whole batch in case there is a bad egg. It's unlikely, but it's better to be sure. Doing this also avoids adding a whole fourth egg if you break the yolk when separating.

3. Carefully whisk the eggs with a fork, incorporating the flour bit by bit until you form a rough dough. If the dough is too dry, you may add a few teaspoons of water. If it's too wet, you may add more flour. Knead until you get a smooth, slightly damp dough, without dry white flour spots in it. You may add more water or flour as you knead. You may also use a stand mixer for this, but I included this in

case you don't have one. Also, it's easier to feel the texture when working with your hands.

4. Form the dough into a smooth ball and wrap it with some plastic wrap. Let it rest on a cutting board or kitchen counter for 30 minutes. After the rest, we will be shaping. If you have a pasta roller and cutter, you may use that. If not, there are other pasta shapes that you can make. Let's make simple ones for the sake of this recipe.

5. To shape, take a rolling pin, or a simple wooden dowel, and flour it. Also, flour your kitchen counter or cutting board. Divide the dough ball into quarters so that it will be easier to work with. Form each quarter into a ball. Take one ball for shaping, and keep the rest under the plastic wrap so that they will not dry out.

6. Flatten the dough ball with your hand first, and then use the rolling pin to get it thin. As you roll out the dough, you may want to rotate it by 90 degrees, and also flip it over several times to get an even sheet. Sprinkle on more flour if it gets too sticky.

7. Once you get a nice thin sheet, sprinkle on a bit more flour. Use a knife to slice a 3-inch-wide strip for lasagna. You can also liberally flour the surface of the

sheet, fold the bottom third toward the middle, then fold it again toward the farthest edge from you, giving you a loosely rolled strip of dough. Cut it perpendicularly, making a quarter of an inch to half an inch per strip. Fluff the strips to open them up, giving you *tagliatelle* or *pappardelle*.

8. Flour the cut pasta to dry out the cut parts. The flour also helps the pasta to dry faster, and prevents it from sticking. You can lay it on dehydrator racks with silicone liners and dry it. You can also hang it on a wire hanger for air drying. For easy portioning, you can flour the strands, and form them into loosely packed nests. Dry until they are stiff and snap when bent.

9. The recipe here is for basic pasta, but you can mix spices and herbs into the dough for a more flavorful and colorful dish.

Proteins

Classic Jerky

This is what pops into the minds of most Americans when you mention dehydrated food. Jerky has been around for a long time, and can be made with pretty much any type of lean meat. For your convenience and affordability, we are going to use classic beef for this recipe.

Ingredients:

❖ 3 lbs. beef, lean

- ❖ 3 tbsp. salt

- ❖ 2 tbsp. honey or brown sugar

- ❖ 1 tbsp. ground black pepper

- ❖ 1 tsp. chili flakes (optional)

- ❖ 1 tsp. liquid smoke

Directions:

1. Save a bit of cash by choosing a whole slab of beef and cut it up yourself at home. Choose a slab coming from the round or flank, as these are very lean cuts. If the slab you have is fresh, trim off any fat or sinew and stash in the freezer for about an hour or two just to stiffen it up a bit to make slicing easier.

2. Slice the beef into strips following the grain of the muscle, about a quarter of an inch thick. Set the meat aside, and mix up the marinade by pouring everything into a thick zip-lock bag. Give it a good mix before adding the meat.

3. Once everything is in the bag, massage it gently to make sure the meat is coated evenly with the marinade.

Place it on a plate or pan in case of any leakage, and place in the fridge overnight.

4. After curing, the strips will become a little bit stiffer since the salt draws out some moisture. Give this a quick rinse to remove excess salt, and lay each piece on a dehydrating rack. Dry with any method you like. As for the texture, it's up to you. Some people like it a bit pliable, and some like it really hard and chewy.

BILTONG

Biltong is an African version of jerky originating from southern countries on the continent. It can consist of various kinds of meat, including kudu, which is a type of antelope. However, if kudu is not available at your local grocery, you can also use beef, pork, turkey, or other game. Aside from salt, biltong is cured with vinegar, which adds tangy taste and kills bacteria.

Ingredients:

❖ 3 lbs. beef, or any other lean meat

❖ 1 oz. vinegar (or any other vinegar that you like)

❖ 1 oz. Worcestershire sauce

- 1 tbsp. sugar or honey

- 1 ½ tbsp. salt

- ½ tsp. pink salt

- 1 ½ tbsp. ground coriander seed

- 2 tsp. ground black pepper

- 2 tsp. ground cumin seeds

- 2 tsp. dried chili flakes

Directions:

1. Buy a whole slab of meat, as lean as possible. Trim off any fat, and if the thickness of the slab is two inches or less, keep it whole. If the slab is really thick, you can slice it along the grain to get one-and-a-half-inch to two-inch-thick slabs.

2. Pat dry the meat with paper towels to remove moisture and transfer it into a zip-lock bag. In a small bowl, mix the Worcestershire sauce, vinegar, salt, pink salt, and sugar. Mix thoroughly, and pour into the zip-lock bag with the meat. Seal, removing as much air as you can, and give

it a gentle massage to coat the pieces. Place in the fridge overnight.

3. Mix the ground coriander, black pepper, cumin, and chili in a small bowl. Take out the meat and drain. There is no need to rinse. Once drained, cover the surface with the spice mix.

4. Air dry the meat, or use a dehydrator until it loses about 50% of its weight. Slice the biltong after drying using a biltong slicer or a knife. Store in airtight containers.

MEAT STICKS

Dried meat is good. But, let's face the facts, it can be quite expensive. I have several recipes here using whole muscle cuts, which you should still try out when you have the budget. However, when you are running a little low on cash, want something meaty, and are not too comfortable with offal yet, then a good alternative is ground meat.

This usually goes cheap since it's easy to process from the butcher's perspective. It also typically contains trimmings from premium cuts. So, the next time you are in your local grocery store, give ground meat a chance.

Ingredients:

❖ 3 lbs. ground meat

❖ 1 ¼ oz. salt

❖ 1 oz. sugar

❖ 1 ¼ tsp. pink salt

❖ ½ cup red wine, or just plain water

❖ 1 tbsp. ground fennel

❖ 1 tbsp. dried thyme

❖ 1 tsp. ground cayenne pepper

❖ 10 feet (3 m) sheep casing, or a ¾" (21 mm) sized collagen casing

Directions:

1. When choosing ground meat, you can use pork, beef, lamb, or even game meats. You can even use chicken, but you need to add a bit of pork to it. The key is to have at least 20% pork fat content; otherwise, the sausage will not form an emulsion. You can also use a mix of ground meat. I usually go for the trifecta of pork, beef, and lamb. Keep the meat cool in the fridge as you set up the rest of your equipment with the wine or water.

2. You can also place it in the freezer if you will be cooking on a different day. Just thaw for about an hour, or just until your stand mixer can handle it. It's imperative to keep things cold when making sausages since you don't want the fat to render and split. Again, all for the emulsion!

3. Bring out a large stand mixer that can accommodate three lbs. of meat. You can also use a large bowl, if you need to mix it by hand. Combine the meat and mix with the rest of the ingredients, except for the wine and the casings. In a different bowl, soak the casing in water to get rid of

the salt, in case of a natural casing, or to rehydrate it, in case of a collagen casing.

4. Use the paddle attachment on your stand mixer, and start it up on low just to get the ground meat loose. Keep it on low, and sprinkle in the spice mix. When fully integrated, slowly pour in the cold wine. Mix until fully integrated and an emulsion is formed.

5. You can tell it's formed when you can take a ball of the mixture and pat it on the palm of your hand without it falling when turned over. You should also see strands and bits of the mixture sticking to the sides of the bowl. You can take a small patty of the mixture and fry it up, so you have an idea of the final flavor, and adjust accordingly.

6. Once your sausage mix is set, store it in the fridge as you set up your sausage stuffer. This recipe makes use of a narrow casing, so use the small stuffer spout. Wet it and slide the casing onto the spout, keeping the end open.

7. Slam the ground meat into the stuffer, so that it does not have air pockets. Push the meat mixture a little bit until you get to the end of the spout. If any part comes out of the spout, you can save it for a meatball later, or open up

your stuffer and drop it in. Pull a bit of the casing and tie a knot.

8. Push the sausage mixture evenly into the casing. You can stuff these a bit fuller than regular sausages since we are not cooking these, we're just drying them. When you have used all of the sausage mixture, or you've run out of casing, form the links by twisting in alternating directions, or use a butcher's twine to separate each link. Use a sausage pricker or a needle and give each sausage link a few stabs. This is to release air pockets and create an outlet where moisture can escape later during the dehydration phase.

9. Arrange your sausage link into two rows and stash them in the fridge overnight. This is for the meat to cure and for the flavors to meld. Doing this in the fridge also dries the surface enough to make the casings sturdy and the link connections completely dry up, so you can snip them off yet still keep the ends of the sausage sealed.

10.	After curing, place the sausage links into your dehydrator or keep them in the fridge to completely dry up. Before you start with the drying phase, remove each link and space them so that they won't be touching each other. If you are using a dehydrator, it can take about 24 hours or so for them to fully dry. If you are air drying, it will take about a few weeks to a month.

TERIYAKI GROUND MEAT JERKY

If you don't want to fuss with casings, like in the meat sticks recipe, follow the fruit leather route and make ground meat jerky. This is a cheaper alternative to regular jerky since it uses ground meat, and lets you create a more uniform product. This recipe has an Asian flair with a teriyaki flavor.

Ingredients:

❖ 3 lbs. ground meat (you can use pork, beef, lamb, or a mixture)

❖ 2/3 cup soy sauce

❖ 1/3 cup Worcestershire sauce

❖ 1/3 cup mirin or sake

❖ 2 tbsp. brown sugar or honey

❖ 1 tbsp. sesame oil

❖ 1 tsp. garlic powder

❖ 1 tsp. ginger powder

❖ 1 tsp. onion powder

Directions:

1. Get a bowl or the work bowl of your stand mixer. Pour in all of the ingredients except for the meat. Whisk well until the sugar is dissolved. Keep the ground meat in the fridge to keep it cold.

2. Add the meat, and mix thoroughly until the mixture becomes very sticky. You can also process this for five minutes in your stand mixer with the paddle attachment.

3. Get a baking sheet the same size as your dehydrator racks, and line it with wax or parchment paper. Place about half a pound of the meat mixture on it, and flatten it a little bit with a spatula. Place another sheet of paper on top and use a rolling pin to flatten the mixture, conforming to the shape of the baking sheet. You should have a single quarter-of-an-inch layer.

4. Remove the top paper sheet, and place the silicone liner over the mixture. Follow it up with an inverted dehydrator rack. Flip the whole thing over, and carefully remove the baking sheet and bottom paper. Reuse the

paper sheets for the remaining meat mixture following the same procedure.

5. Place the racks into your dehydrator, and dry as you would with jerky. It should be stiff enough to hold its shape, but not so dry that it crumbles when bent. Just remove the jerky sheets and cut them up into strips.

DUCK PROSCIUTTO

In Italy, prosciutto is usually made of a whole hind leg of pork, air-dried for a year or more. This takes time, commitment and some dedication to make. Why don't we make things simple and use a smaller and cheaper piece of meat-- duck breasts!

Ingredients:

❖ 1 lb. duck breasts, boneless, with skin on

❖ Salt

❖ Ground black pepper

Directions:

1. Get a container for salt boxing. The container should have enough space to fit the breast, with space on the sides

for the salt. If you are using two or more breasts, the container should have enough space for the breasts, without them touching each other. Make sure it's clean and dry, then set it aside.

2. Pat the breasts dry, and score the skin for water to come out and salt to get in. Pour an even layer of salt, about half an inch thick, on the bottom of the container. Lay down the breasts, making sure that they are not touching each other, and not touching the sides of the container.

3. Sprinkle more salt to completely cover the breasts by about an inch. Make sure there is no space where salt is not touching the duck. Cover the container, and place in the fridge for 24 hours.

4. After curing, remove the duck breasts. They should be a bit stiff at this point. Rinse well, and pat dry with paper towels. Cover all the surface area of the duck breasts with ground black pepper for flavor, and serve as a protective barrier to keep out mold and bacteria. Dry it until completely stiff, or until the total weight is reduced by half.

DRY-CURED EGG

Continuing with the fowl theme, why not preserve eggs as well? They are rich in protein and fat, and smaller--perfect for those who are trying out dry curing.

Ingredients:

❖ Egg yolk

❖ Salt

❖ Dried herbs (of your choice)

❖ Ground spice (of your choice)

Directions:

1. Clean a small plastic container that can fit an egg yolk. You can also cure two or more yolks at a time, just as long as you have a container that can fit them without touching each other.

2. Mix the salt, herbs, and spices in a small bowl. Mix enough to salt box the yolk, so estimate accordingly.

3. Pour enough of the salt mixture into the container to form a layer half an inch thick. Make a slight indentation in the salt layer using a spoon, or the egg itself.

4. Crack the egg, and separate the yolk into a separate small bowl. This makes it easier to lay it down onto the salt bed, and as a temporary area to check if the yolk breaks. If it's whole, slowly transfer the yolk onto the salt bed.

5. Cover with more of the salt mixture and place in the fridge overnight, or until the yolk becomes solid and stiff.

6. Excavate the yolk, and rinse off any excess salt. Dry the yolk until completely solid and until it deepens in color. To serve, finely grate it over pasta or bruschetta.

DRIED FISH

This is one of the oldest dried foods made. Jesus even shared dried fish with his disciples. This is great for store-bought fish, or for processing what you caught on your fishing trip. This is an easy recipe, which concentrates more on process rather than exact measurements.

Ingredients:

❖ Fish (you can use cod, mackerel, sardines, or whatever is fresh, cheap, and good in your area)

❖ Salt

❖ Water

Directions:

1. Begin preparing your fish by removing the scales. If they are small enough, you can open up the belly to remove the organs and gills. If they are thick, you can slice them along the dorsal fin, going through the spine but keeping the belly intact, so that you butterfly the fish. If they are quite large, cut them into fillets or steaks.

2. Wash off any organs and blood. Use fish tweezers to remove any pin bones that may have been left behind. Place them in a container with about an inch of headroom.

3. Make a brine by mixing three parts water and one part salt in a bowl or pitcher. Mix thoroughly until the salt is dissolved. Pour and cover the fish pieces by about half an inch. In case the fish pieces float, you may weigh them down with a plate. Leave this brine in the fridge overnight.

4. Carefully remove the fish pieces from the brine, and pat dry with paper towels. Lay them flat on your dehydrator rack, and dry until the meat is stiff. You can do this same recipe with cephalopods like squid, and soft-shelled crustaceans like prawns and shrimp.

BOTTARGA

Remember the dry-cured eggs? Well, don't think dry-cure only works for chicken or other fowl eggs-- you can also use the method on other eggs, too. The Italians love cured fish eggs to make a stew or pasta dishes.

Ingredients:

❖ Fish roe in the sac (you may use the roe from cod, mullet, shad, or trout)

❖ Salt

Directions:

1. Clean a plastic container that can fit the roe sacs without them touching each other.

2. Make an even layer of salt at the bottom, about half an inch thick. Gently lay down the delicate roe sacs on the salt, and cover them with more salt. Make sure the fish eggs are completely covered by about half an inch and the surface is in contact with salt. Store this in the fridge for 24 hours.

3. After curing, they should feel stiffer. If not, leave them in for a few hours more. When they are ready, excavate and give them a quick rinse to remove the excess salt.

4. Dry them for a week or two until completely stiff and crumbly. They are great grated over some oil, pasta, and a bit of pasta water.

Now that you have all this dried food, you will have to store it. The shelf life-extending power of drying is only as successful as how it is stored. Even if you have removed as much moisture as you can, it can creep back in, bringing nasty bacteria with it and spoiling your dried food.

First, let's talk about the estimated shelf life of dried goods, as specified by the USDA and the National Center for Home Food Preservation (NCHFP).

✓ For uncured meats, the shelf life is one to two months, but can be extended to six months by vacuum sealing and storing in the freezer.

✓ Grains, beans, and rice can last for a whole year in a dry container.

✓ Fruits can last up to a year, as long as they are stored at a 60°F temperature or lower. You can extend this further by vacuum sealing.

✓ Fruit leather can be stored for one or two months at room temperature, but can last up to a year in the freezer.

✓ Vegetables can last up to six months in the fridge, or an ambient temperature of 60°F or lower. You can extend this further by vacuum sealing.

Now, keep in mind that these are suggested shelf lives. You can actually extend them further, depending on storage conditions. Also, since you are drying your own food, you'll develop a sense of things to look for that make dried food inedible. So, use your experience to make an informed judgment. Here are some tips on storing your dried food and fully extending shelf life.

✓ When the food is still warm from the dehydrator, let it completely cool to room temperature before transferring it to a container. The moisture is still in motion because of the heat, and can cause condensation when inside a sealed container.

✓ Fruits have a lot of moisture inside them, and even after dehydrating, there can be some portions or spots within them that have moisture pockets. The NCHFP suggests conditioning them first, before placing them in long-term storage. Conditioning dried fruits allows for any moisture that is left to redistribute within the morsel, so it can be released when it reaches the warm and dry parts. To condition, let them completely cool to room temperature and then store them in a glass jar for a week. If any condensation or signs of moisture appear, just dry them for another hour or two in the dryer.

✓ Do not use zip-lock bags when storing at room temperature. These bags are not airtight, and air can still get in as you open and close them. The bags can also touch the surface of the food, transferring any condensation that may form inside. If you are going to take a piece of dried food every once in a while, store it in airtight glass jars, and place them away from sunlight or in your fridge.

✓ Oxidation is the chemical process that occurs when other compounds or substances come into contact with oxygen, which causes hydrogen ions to be released. This makes the compounds unstable and degrade after further exposure. This is the same reaction that causes cut apples to turn brown, creates rust, and makes bread go stale. That is why an airtight container is best, as it protects dried food from oxygen.

✓ A vacuum sealer is the optimum food storage tool. Airtight containers keep out air, but you are then stuck with the air you have trapped inside. With a vacuum sealer, you can get rid of any air in the bags or jars. That is why you will not have to worry about the bag touching the surface of the food, since there is no air for the bacteria to breathe in and grow. Since there is no air, you will not have to worry about your food degrading over time. Vacuum sealing has two primary forms:

o Vacuum bags are more well-known, as most use vacuum bags as packaging for frozen goods in grocery stores. The whole process is very simple. Just place the food in specially made vacuum bags. The vacuum sealer will suck all of the air out, shrinking the bag around the food, leaving no space for air, and then sealing everything.

o It's easy to vacuum-seal portioned dried goods. You can store them in the freezer or in the fridge, which is great for meal prepping or scheduled meals. However, the bags will have to be cut open, making them not very reusable. And they generate waste.

o Most vacuum sealers have a small spout or outlet, to which you can attach a hose. This is used to vacuum-seal jars. Some manufacturers use specific jars for vacuum sealing, while some manufacture a special adapter that you can use on mason jars. Because of the rigid nature of jars, compared to plastic bags, the vacuum causes negative pressure. So, don't be surprised when you hear a popping sound whenever you open up a vacuum jar, as the air rushes in and fills the void. Vacuum-sealed jars are a better option for batch storage of dried goods. These are also reusable and resealable, so you can pop one open, take out the portion that you like, and just vacuum seal it back up. The jars are quite an investment though, and can be quite bulky to store. You also have a risk of dropping and breaking jars.

✓ If you want things to be a bit more formal, and if you want a single packaging for reheating, consider using Mylar® bags. These are made of plastic and thin sheets of aluminum for strength and serve as a barrier against oxygen. A plastic bag may seem solid, but it does allow a bit of air and oxygen in, which is detrimental to dried goods.

✓ The opaque surface gives your dry goods protection from sunlight. Once properly vacuum-sealed, Mylar® bags are ready for long-term storage. Mylar® bags are also ideal since some have high heat ratings, which means that they have a higher aluminum content. When you have a high heat rating, you can pour hot water straight into the bag to rehydrate and warm up dried goods, creating a warm meal while hiking or camping.

✓ Whenever you seal something up for storage, you can add an additional safety net by including small packets of desiccant packs or oxygen absorbers with the food. Some may view this as redundant, but I would rather err on the side of caution.

✓ Desiccant packs or silica gel packets absorb moisture in the air and keep it away from your food. Oxygen absorbers can contain ferrous carbonate, sodium hydrogen carbonate, or ascorbate. As the name suggests, these only react with and absorb oxygen. These are usually used for dried goods that are not vacuum-sealed.

THE CARBON FOOTPRINT

According to a 2022 study conducted by the Rhodium Group, an independent environmental research organization the United States recorded an increase of 1.3% in greenhouse gas (GHG) emissions. It would seem that the rate of emission rebounded from the 10.6% drop in 2020, and it does not look like we will be able to achieve the 50% to 52% drop from the 2005 levels by 2030 as stated in the Paris Agreement.

This is a big undertaking, and each of us must do our part not just in helping our country, but also the global environment as a whole. This means that we have to do more than just attain food sustainability and go beyond it, but still remain within our means. Here are some cheap and manageable ways to lower your carbon footprint outside of food sustainability.

✓ Use reusable bags when shopping. It saves you from having plastic waste, and it's easy to fold up and carry in your bag. I usually bring two or three with me wherever I go, just in case I have to buy something. They are sturdy too, so you won't have to worry about the bottom of your bag suddenly giving out sharp or bulky items.

✓ When you are shopping for something, look for items made with recycled materials. You do not need toilet paper from virgin pulp if you are just going to wipe with it and throw it in the toilet. There is no shame in using recycled products, as long as they can perform their function well. There is also no shame in buying second-hand items. Ask your relatives, neighbors, or friends for some hand-me-down clothes or other goods. You will find that some folks are more than willing to get rid of items that they are no longer using.

✓ Speaking of hand-me-downs, the United States Environmental Protection agency (EPA) reports that out of the estimated 17 million tons of textile and clothing manufactured in 2018, only around 2 million tons were recycled, and 3 million tons were incinerated for energy recovery. A whopping 11 million tons ended up in landfills. This trend continues to rise, even until today.

✓ That is a lot of wasted materials and waste. The whole textile industry is calculated to be responsible for about 10% of global GHG emissions. So, to do our part, try to make the most out of the clothes that you have. So, what if they are really loose or have holes in them? You can still wear them at home, or turn them into rags so you won't have to buy any. You can also donate clothes to charity organizations, so that you can clear out the closet and extend the use of your clothes. Also, don't buy into fleeting fashion trends. Find a look that is decent and works for you, and stick to it.

✓ Wash your clothes in cold water, and use detergents that are best used with cold water as well. Minimize the use of hot water for washing clothes as much as you can. You can cut back on your carbon footprint by about 500 pounds a year if you just do your laundry with cold water.

✓ Keeping water hot consumes a lot of energy. I do understand that it gets cold during early mornings or in winter, so I won't ask you to stop using your water heater. You can, however, just turn it down a little. Maintaining a 120°F for your warm water temperature is fine for baths and showers. It's said that keeping at this temperature can save you over 500 pounds of CO_2 per year.

✓ In line with this, learn not to stray far from the ambient temperature when adjusting the thermostat of your air conditioner. The compressor or inverter exerts a lot of effort when keeping the house cold during summer, and hot during winter. The more it strains, the more energy it consumes, and it all adds to your bill. It also causes the motor to degrade faster, causing it to work inefficiently. The U.S. Department of Energy (DOE) suggests keeping your indoor air temperature to about 20°F above or below the outdoor air temperature. You should also adjust your thermostat depending on the time of day, as the ambient temperature changes. Doing this can decrease bills.

✓ When you are in the market for new appliances or electronics, choose the ones that are eco-friendly and energy efficient. Most of these will have the Energy Star certification and label to indicate that they are, indeed, energy-efficient based on EPA standards. These products will not only be relatively good for the environment, but will actually save you some cash in the long run.

✓ If you still haven't done so, you should switch out your incandescent light bulbs into LED bulbs right now! These are not only more environmentally friendly to manufacture, but they also use less energy for the amount of light emitted, thus saving you money on your electric bill. They also last longer than incandescent light bulbs.

✓ Speaking of bills, do try to check your utility lines. Do this by temporarily shutting off your circuit breakers, your main waterline, and other utilities. Then, look for the corresponding meters for these, and check for activity. If something is still running despite turning everything off, it indicates a leak, wiretaps, or connections that are running without your knowledge. Either way, you are losing some cash while the utility is being wasted, or stolen. Check your lines once in a while to make sure things are running smoothly.

✓ The use of cars becomes less energy-efficient if you only drive yourself to and from the office. Consider starting a carpool group with your office mates or setting up a rideshare program with someone that goes to almost the same areas as you do in your daily routine. If you are in the market for a new car, go check out hybrid or fully electric cars.

✓ If the car you own has a conventional combustion engine, or buying a new electric car is not in the picture, then keep your engine well-maintained. Some parts will naturally degrade over time, and this will lead to inefficient combustion, and more pollution. Look for suggestions from trustworthy mechanics. Do not ignore that engine light, and check your parking area for any oil leaks that should be addressed immediately.

✓ If you don't have a car, you can commute, which is considerably cheaper than a car. Commuting allows for more passengers to occupy a vehicle space on the road. Commuting also cuts back on overall fuel consumption compared to driving alone in a car, since you are able to transport more people with a single vehicle.

✓ If a crowded bus or train is not up your alley, then you can buy a bike. Bikes are cheap, and they use your own strength for fuel. Biking to work is literally a spin class while on the move. Just bring your work clothes in a bag for a quick change, and brush up on road rules and road etiquette.

✓ Having a total 0-carbon footprint is a dream that every environmentally conscious person has. If you really can't lower your carbon footprint due to circumstances, and have some money to spare, try looking into carbon offset apps or organizations. Carbon offset is donating money to fund eco-friendly and sustainable projects, thereby offsetting your carbon footprint by lowering it somewhere else, or with a different action.

A Dry Farewell

Climate change is happening whether we like it or not, and whether we believe in it or not. Climate change affects us all and you can already feel its effects on our food supply. Prices are slowly going up; plus, you often see news about supply shortages nowadays.

This just means that times are changing, and so should we. We have grown accustomed to purchasing and eating habits that may have been fine before, but they are actually slowly proving to be unsustainable.

Simply changing a few things within our home helps with this global problem. By doing the simple suggestions I have written down in this book, you can do your part and help things improve in the long run. Plus, there is no stopping you from striving for food sustainability, as there is no downside to it.

You are doing your part to help the environment, and at the same time, having a fruitful food supply that can last a long time. You can even save some money in doing so. Food is a key element of life, and any problems relating to it should be one of our top priorities, if not the first thing we should be addressing.

It's my hope that this book serves as a wake-up call for people to think about what they put into their mouths, how they get it, and how other people get theirs. Some people work hard just to have a taste of the good stuff, while others work just as hard just to have enough food to sustain them from paycheck to paycheck.

It's a universal struggle that we contend with every single day, and will be continuously contending with until we leave this earth.

I hope that with this book, I've imparted to you the notion that striving for food sustainability, or at least learning about food preservation, will give us less to worry about in our already busy and worrisome lives.

Made in the USA
Las Vegas, NV
27 November 2023

81691580R00069